A New True Book

SKUNKS

By Emilie U. Lepthien

CHILDRENS PRESS®
CHICAGO

Young skunk
smelling a flower

PHOTO CREDITS

© Alan & Sandy Carey—2, 34, 35, 36, 37

Photri—© B. E. White, 44

Root Resources—© C. Postmus, 8 (bottom left);
© Anthony Mercieca, 12; © Robert Campbell, 13; © Jan
L. Wassink, 29, 30; © Mary & Lloyd McCarthy, 43

Tom Stack & Associates—© Thomas Kitchin, 8
(bottom right), 18; © Larry Brock, 17, 22, 45; © Gary
Milburn, 21; © Wendy Shattil & Robert Rozinski, 23;
© Brian Parker, 40

SuperStock International, Inc.—© J. Warden, 8 (top
left); © A. Mercieca, 14; © H. Morton, 39

Valan—© Jeff Foott, Cover, 27; © Murray O'Neill, 4;
© Wayne Lankinen, 8 (top right), 10, 38 (bottom),
© James D. Markou, 38 (top)

Visuals Unlimited—© Joe McDonald, 7, 16, 25; © W. A.
Banaszewski, 19; © Wiliam J. Weber, 24; © Tom J.
Ulrich, 26; © Daphne Kinzler, 33

Cover: Striped skunk mother with babies

Project Editor: Fran Dyra
Design: Margrit Fiddle

Library of Congress Cataloging-in-Publication Data

Lepthien, Emilie U. (Emilie Utteg)
  Skunks / by Emilie U. Lepthien.
    p.   cm. — (A New true book)
  Includes index.
  Summary: Provides detailed descriptions of the
physical characteristics and habits of skunks.
  ISBN 0-516-01197-9
  1. Skunks—Juvenile literature.
[1. Skunks.] I. Title.
QL737.C25L47 1993
599.74'447—dc20   93-3410
                          CIP
                          AC

TABLE OF CONTENTS

AN UNPOPULAR ANIMAL

Why do people dislike skunks? Skunks are beautiful animals. They have glossy black-and-white fur coats. They have big, bushy tails. They rarely eat farm animals. And they don't destroy property.

But most people don't like skunks. Why?

Skunks have a powerful weapon. They give off a terrible smell!

Opposite page: Striped skunks live in many places in North America.

When a skunk is angry or afraid, it can release a spray of terrible-smelling liquid called musk. The musk comes from two glands near the base of the skunk's tail. This powerful odor can be smelled almost 1 mile (1.6 kilometers) away. It can last for days on whatever has been sprayed.

WHAT IS A SKUNK?

Skunks are mammals.
They belong to the weasel
family, which includes

Skunk relatives include (clockwise from top left) badgers, otters, martens, and weasels.

mink, otters, badgers, wolverines, weasels, martens, and fishers. All these animals have musk glands. But only skunks use musk as a defense.

8

The name "skunk"
comes from the Algonquian
word *segonku.* Some
people have given skunks
other names: polecats,
woodpussies, and the
French-Canadian name
enfant du diable, which
means "child of the devil."

There are four kinds of
skunks. They are found
only in the Western
Hemisphere.

The striped skunk lives
throughout the United
States and in southern

Striped skunk

Canada. It is the most
common skunk in the
United States.

A narrow white stripe
runs down the middle of

its face. The back of its head is white, and two white stripes form a V shape down its back.

Striped skunks grow about as big as a cat— from 13 to 18 inches (33 to 46 centimeters) long. The tail adds another 7 to 10 inches (18 to 25 centimeters).

The striped skunk's scientific name is *Mephitis mephitis,* which means "terrible smell" and says it not once but twice.

The spotted skunk lives
in the western United States
and Mexico. It has spots of
white fur all over its body.
Spotted skunks are smaller
than striped skunks.

Spotted skunk

Hog-nosed skunk

Hog-nosed skunks are found from the southwestern United States to the tip of South America. Their broad, hairless nose looks a little like a pig's snout.

The hooded skunk is found in a small area of the southwestern United States and in Central America. It has long hair around its neck.

Hooded skunk

SKUNK HOMES

Skunks live in underground homes called dens. They line the den with dried leaves and grasses to make a cozy nest.

Skunks may dig their own den or move into one dug by another animal. Sometimes they make a

These striped skunks have made a den in a hollow log.

den in a hollow log or
under a house or barn.
    Two or three females may
share a den, but each
male has its own den.
    Skunks do not hibernate,
or sleep through the

winter. They stay warm and dry by sleeping through the coldest days and nights. But their body temperature does not drop as it does in hibernating animals. If there is even a short warm spell, skunks wake up and go out to search for food.

Skunks may leave their dens in winter to search for food.

17

The skunk's strong claws are just right for digging.

SHARP CLAWS, SHORT LEGS

A skunk has five toes on each foot. Each toe on the front feet has a sharp, curved claw, used for digging. The claws on the

18

Skunks can run fast for short distances.

hind feet are also sharp.

Skunks have short legs,
so they can't run very fast.
They can run at about 9
miles (14 kilometers) an
hour for short distances.
But usually they walk slowly.
They stop often to dig for
worms or grubs with their
sharp-clawed front feet.

SEEING, SMELLING, AND HEARING

Skunks are nocturnal animals. This means that they are usually active at night. During the day they sleep in their dens.

Skunks can see quite well close up, even at night. But they cannot see well at distances beyond 20 feet (6 meters).

They use their keen senses of smell and hearing to find worms and

Skunks use their keen senses
to help them find food.

grubs under the ground.
Their sharp hearing also
helps warn them of danger.
  Skunks make a variety
of sounds. They squeak,
hiss, screech, and coo.
When hunting for food, they
make a soft snuffing noise.

Skunks have sharp teeth.

SHARP TEETH

Striped skunks have thirty-four teeth. They have twelve very sharp incisors, or cutting teeth, in the front of their jaws. Skunks can kill small animals and snakes with a single bite on the neck or head. They use their back teeth for chewing.

A SMELLY ATTACK

When a skunk is angry or afraid, it sprays the enemy with its musk. But first it gives a warning—it stamps its feet, arches its back, and hisses.

If the warning is ignored, the striped skunk curls into a U shape and raises its tail straight up.

Striped skunk warning the photographer—stay away. Skunks can fire their musk glands five or six times very rapidly.

The muscles around the musk glands contract, and two jets of oily, yellowish musk shoot out.

The spotted skunk stands on its front feet

The spotted skunk stands on its front feet to warn that it is about to spray.

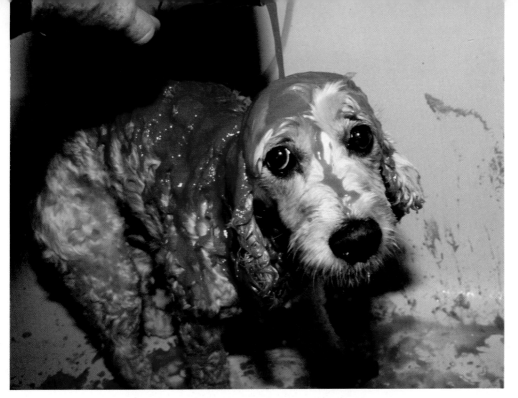

A dog that has been sprayed by a skunk may be washed with tomato juice. This helps get rid of the awful odor.

and sprays the musk forward over its back.

Liquid musk can travel as far as 12 feet (4 meters). The musk covers a large area when it breaks into a fine mist.

FINDING FOOD

Skunks eat almost anything. They catch snakes and small rodents such as mice. But insects are their favorite food. They eat grasshoppers, spiders, weevils, grubs,

A striped skunk looks over some mushrooms. Are they food?

Skunks like to eat the eggs of birds and turtles.

caterpillars, and crickets.
They also eat fruits,
vegetables, frogs, and
bird and turtle eggs.

Occasionally, they may
kill a chicken or steal an
egg. But farmers know that
skunks keep down pests
such as insects and mice.

A NEW FAMILY

In spring, male skunks leave their dens to find a mate. They may travel a long distance, usually at night. If two males choose the same female, they may fight. They may even spray each other with musk.

Mating takes place in March. The male and female stay together for a short time. Then the female drives the male

A striped skunk mother with her tiny kitten

away. He may never see the female again, and he will not know his own offspring.

The mother-to-be lines a den with soft grass and leaves. There, in early May, the baby skunks, called kittens, are born.

Striped skunk kittens

A litter usually has six kittens. At birth, the kittens weigh about 1 ounce (28 grams) and are only 3 to 4 inches (7.6 to 10 centimeters) long.

The newborn kittens can neither see nor hear. They have no teeth. They have a thin coat of hair in the black-and-white pattern of their parents' fur.

Within 30 minutes of their birth, the kittens begin to feed on mother's milk. They grow quickly. After three weeks they weigh 6 to 7 ounces (170 to 198 grams), and they can see and hear.

When the kittens are old enough to eat solid food, the mother brings them insects.

A baby skunk raises its tail in warning. But nothing happens because its musk glands are not developed yet.

The kittens practice raising their tails to spray. But their musk glands do not develop until they are about six weeks old and are ready to leave the den.

A skunk family takes a walk.

The mother skunk leads the kittens out of the den and teaches them how to catch food. She also shows them how to defend themselves.

The mother skunk teaches her kittens how to live outside the den.

By late summer the male kittens begin to go off on their own. The female kittens remain with the mother a little longer.

The bobcat (above) and the fox (below) sometimes prey on skunks.

SKUNK ENEMIES

Great horned owl

Most animals learn to avoid skunks because they can't stand the smell of musk. But the great horned owl, the fox, and the bobcat sometimes catch skunks.

39

Skunk raiding
a garbage can

Skunks prefer to live in woodland areas, but some find homes in towns and suburban areas. Many of these slow-moving animals are killed by automobiles.

A USEFUL ODOR

Scientists use chemicals to produce a skunk-like odor. They put these chemicals into pipelines carrying natural gas. Because natural gas has no smell and no color, a leak in a pipeline might not be noticed. It could cause an explosion. But adding a terrible odor to natural gas makes a leak easy to detect.

VALUABLE ANIMALS

In the past, great
numbers of striped skunks
were trapped each year.
Their fur was used to
make coats and jackets.
The fur was called Alaskan
sable or black marten. But
when a new law required
honest labels on clothing,

The beautiful fur of the skunk was often made into coats
and jackets under the names Alaskan sable or black marten.

skunk coats lost their
appeal. Sales dropped,
and the skunk was saved
from possible extinction.

SKUNKS TODAY

There are probably more skunks in North America today than there were when the European settlers landed more than 350 years ago.

Spotted skunk

Skunks have learned to adapt to changes in their environment. They are clever and interesting animals. Maybe they don't mind being unpopular.

45

WORDS YOU SHOULD KNOW

active (AK • tiv) — moving around

adapt (uh • DAPT) — to change to fit new conditions

chemicals (KEM • ih • kilz) — materials that can be combined to make substances like those that are found in nature

contract (kahn • TRAKT) — to squeeze; to pull together

cozy (KOH • zee) — warm and comfortable

environment (en • VY • run • mint) — the things that surround a plant or an animal; the lands and waters of the earth

extinction (ex • TINK • shun) — dying out

gland (GLAND) — a special body part that makes things that the body can use or give off

grubs (GRUHBZ) — small, wormlike animals

hibernate (HY • ber • nait) — to go into a state of deep sleep in which body temperature drops and breathing slows

incisors (in • SY • zerz) — long, sharp front teeth

litter (LIH • ter) — a group of baby animals born at the same time to the same mother

mammal (MAM • il) — one of a group of warm-blooded animals that have hair and nurse their young with milk

Mephitis mephitis (meh • FIH • tiss meh • FIH • tiss) — the scientific name for the striped skunk, meaning "terrible smell"

musk (MUHSK) — a substance with a strong and lasting odor

nocturnal (nok • TER • nil) — moving around at night

pipeline (PYPE • lyne) — a long pipe that carries such things as gas or oil for great distances

prey (PRAY) — to hunt other animals for food

rodent (ROH • dint) — an animal that has long, sharp front teeth for gnawing

scientific name (sye • en • TIH • fik NAIM) — a name, usually from the Latin language, that scientists give to a plant or an animal

settlers (SET • lerz) — people who come to a new country and establish farms or other homes there

unpopular (un • PAH • pyoo • ler) — not well liked

INDEX

About the Author

Emilie U. Lepthien received her BA and MS degrees and certificate in school administration from Northwestern University. She taught upper-grade science and social studies, wrote and narrated science programs for the Chicago Public Schools' station WBEZ, and was principal in Chicago, Illinois, for twenty years. She received the American Educator's Medal from Freedoms Foundation.

She is a member of Delta Kappa Gamma Society International, Chicago Principals' Association, Illinois Women's Press Association, National Federation of Press Women, and AAUW.

She has written books in the Enchantment of the World, New True Books, and America the Beautiful series.